The BIG PICTURE

The Design & Formatting of Large-Format Digital Printing

From the Publishers of *The Big Picture* Magazine

ST MEDIA GROUP INTERNATIONAL

Cincinnati, Ohio

Hardcover ISBN: 0-944094-42-2
Paperback ISBN: 0-8230-0548-8

Published by:
ST Books
ST Media Group International Inc.
407 Gilbert Avenue
Cincinnati, Ohio 45202
Tel. 513-421-2050
Fax 513-421-6110
E-mail: books@stmediagroup.com
www.stmediagroup.com

Distributed to the book and art trade in the U.S. and Canada by:
Watson-Guptill Publications
770 Broadway
New York, NY 10003

Distributed to the book and art trade outside the U.S. and Canada by:
HarperCollins International
10 East 53rd Street
New York, NY 10022-5229

Book design by Jeff Russ, Sr. Art Director, *Signs of the Times*

Book compiled by:
Mark Kissling
Susan Patton
Eileen Fritsch
Heather Gaynor
Linda Kitchen
Kacey King

Printed in China

10 9 8 7 6 5 4 3 2 1

CONTENTS

THE BIG PICTURE

Creative possibilities without limits....
Over the past 10 years, advances in large-format digital printing technology have made it economically feasible to produce large, full-color, photorealistic graphics in quantities as small as a single print. Simultaneous advances in computing power, scanners, and graphics-fabrication materials have made it possible to create these graphics for a variety of surfaces, environments, and requirements.

Simply put: Providers of large-format digital printing services can now execute almost any creative concept a designer can dream up--at prices that even small-town businesses can afford.

On the following pages, *The Big Picture* magazine is proud to present just a few examples of how large graphics are changing the visual landscape around the world. You'll see how big graphics are being used to solve challenges in brand marketing, retailing, promotions, exhibitions, wayfinding, fine art, and interior decor.

We hope some of the inspiring examples shown on these pages will help solve challenges facing clients of your own.

For continuing coverage of other exciting applications, and assistance in finding qualified suppliers, turn to *The Big Picture* magazine and visit www.bigpicture.net

Acknowledgements
ST Media Group International would like to thank all of our friends in the large-format digital graphics field who contributed photographs that made this book possible. For a list of companies involved in designing and producing the graphics featured in this book, see p. 164.

The Big Picture editorial staff also wishes to thank staff members from our sister publications at ST Media Group International—*Signs of the Times* and *VM+SD* (Visual Merchandising + Store Design)—who generously contributed case study ideas, editorial support, and art direction.

WALLSCAPES & BEYOND

Along well-traveled highways and city streets, conventional billboard space has become increasingly scarce and expensive. As a result, many companies now use "wallscapes" on the windows and sides of their buildings to promote their businesses, products, or special events.

Colorful, artfully created wallscapes are also adding promotional value to construction-site fences and barriers, covering up rundown, abandoned buildings, and creating distinctive environments for trade shows.

Some of these building "spectaculars" are created as 10 to 16-ft wide strips on "superwide" inkjet printers. For these types of applications, images are printed on vinyl mesh or other lightweight fabrics that allow wind to pass through.

Other wallscapes are actually a jigsaw puzzle-like assembly of smaller, numbered panels that are adhered to the windows of a building. Window-mounted wallscapes use a special, perforated vinyl material that enables building occupants to continue to see out the graphics-covered windows.

PROJECT: E.T. Anniversary Building Wrap, Hollywood, CA
PRODUCTION: Adera Corp., Las Vegas, NV, SkyTag, Beverly Hills, CA
PRINTING DEVICE: Vutek UltraVu 3360 superwide inkjet

To celebrate the 20th anniversary re-release of the film *E.T., The Extra-Terrestrial*, Universal Studios commissioned the SkyTag outdoor-media company to produce blockbuster building murals. This three-sided building wrap was applied to the windows of the 7080 Hollywood Boulevard Building at the corner of Hollywood and LaBrea. Adera Corp. output the graphics on Clear Focus SuperVue™ perforated window-graphics film, which enables building occupants to continue to see out of the windows.

PROJECT: City Hall Scaffolding Graphics, Graz, Austria
PRODUCTION: Typico Megaprints GmbH and Co.
PRINTING DEVICE: Proprietary superwide airbrush

The capital building in Graz, Austria was home to some of the world's biggest political cartoons, when construction scaffolding was draped with this 222.96 sq m vinyl-mesh mural depicting well-known Austrians, such as Arnold Schwarzenegger (center).

PROJECT: Pokémon Welcome Banner, Long Beach, CA
PRODUCTION: AAA Flag and Banner Mfg. Co., Los Angeles, CA
PRINTING DEVICE: Vutek UltraVu 5300 superwide inkjet

Big, bright and colorful banners are often used to create excitement and greet attendees at venues hosting special events. This wallscape and entranceway canopy welcomed Pokémon trading card enthusiasts to the Super Trainer Showdown held aboard the RMS Queen Mary, docked at Long Beach, CA.

PROJECT: Construction Graphics at The Setai Luxury Resort, Miami Beach, FL
PRODUCTION: Sungraf Inc., Hallandale, FL
PRINTING DEVICE: NUR Salsa superwide inkjet

While the 40-story, oceanfront Setai Luxury Resort Hotel and Condominium complex was being built, the plain, plywood barrier surrounding the site was dressed up with graphics. The images conveyed the upscale nature of the complex and generated interest in leasing.

Ceremonial-mask graphics in various sizes were output on Sungraf's 5-m (16.4-ft) inkjet printer onto 18-oz. matte banner material from Tubelite. The largest graphic was a mural-size print that was 3.2 m high and 34 m long (10.5 ft x 111.6 ft). To keep the visuals from being scarred by graffiti, the pedestrian-level graphics were protected with a DuPont™ Teflon® overlaminate from Avery Dennison. Sungraf used a painted wood trim to cover up where the printed vinyl was stapled to the plywood barrier.

Photos of installations in Italy by Blue Bianco (Milano). Foto Berti (Pistoia), and A. Bornaghi (Firenze)

PROJECT: Alfa Romeo Banner, Italy, commissioned by B.A.D. Publicity
PRODUCTION: eXtraLarge Italia, division of Vertical Vision International
PRINTING DEVICE: NUR Blueboard superwide inkjet

The wallscapes shown here and through page 25 dramatically illustrate the raw power of huge visuals and the versatility of this new form of outdoor advertising. Unlike conventional billboards, wallscapes aren't limited to standard dimensions or sizes, but can be configured to match whatever space is available in population-dense or high-traffic locations.

On historic buildings throughout Europe undergoing renovation projects, eXtraLarge has placed advertisements that help disguise the construction scaffolding.

To serve the global brand-marketing needs of multinational companies, eXtraLarge is part of Vertical Vision International, which has offices in the US, Germany, the Netherlands, the UK, and Italy. Vertical Vision also offers large-format graphics for trade-show, retail, fleet, and specialty applications.

PROJECT: Algida Magnum Double Schockolate Billboard, Italy, commissioned by Wall System
PRODUCTION: eXtraLarge Italia, division of Vertical Vision International
PRINTING DEVICE: NUR Blueboard superwide inkjet

PROJECT: Calvin Klein Jeans Wall Wrap, Italy, commissioned by Externa
PRODUCTION: eXtraLarge Italia, division of Vertical Vision International
PRINTING DEVICE: NUR Blueboard superwide inkjet

PROJECT: La Superbia Building Wrap, Italy, commissioned by Wall System
PRODUCTION: eXtraLarge Italia, division of Vertical Vision International
PRINTING DEVICE: NUR Blueboard superwide inkjet

PROJECT: Seiko Billboard, Italy, commissioned by Externa
PRODUCTION: eXtraLarge Italia, division of Vertical Vision International
PRINTING DEVICE: NUR Blueboard superwide inkjet

Photo credit: Ziv Karen

PROJECT: Castro Wallscape, Israel, commissioned by BARAM Original Advertising
PRODUCTION: eXtraLarge Italia, division of Vertical Vision International
PRINTING DEVICE: NUR Blueboard superwide inkjet

PROJECT: Wyler Vetta Billboard, Italy, commissioned by Wall System
PRODUCTION: eXtraLarge Italia, division of Vertical Vision International
PRINTING DEVICE: NUR Blueboard superwide inkjet

PROJECT: Breil Billboard, Italy, commissioned by Wall System
PRODUCTION: eXtraLarge Italia, division of Vertical Vision International
PRINTING DEVICE: NUR Blueboard superwide inkjet

PROJECT: Posteitaliane Wall Coverings, Italy, commissioned by Wall System
PRODUCTION: eXtraLarge Italia, division of Vertical Vision International
PRINTING DEVICE: NUR Blueboard superwide inkjet

PROJECT: Versace Wallscape, Italy, commissioned by Elle Cart Trading
PRODUCTION: eXtraLarge Italia, division of Vertical Vision International
PRINTING DEVICE: NUR Blueboard superwide inkjet

PROJECT: Valtur Superlarge Building Wrap, Italy, commissioned by Wall System
PRODUCTION: eXtraLarge Italia, division of Vertical Vision International
PRINTING DEVICE: NUR Blueboard superwide inkjet

PROJECT: Bayer Headquarters Wrap, Leverkusen, Germany
PRODUCTION: Makom/M.NUR, Kassel, Germany
PRINTING DEVICE: NUR Blueboard superwide inkjet

The pharmaceuticals firm Bayer attracted worldwide attention for its centennial celebration by creating an aspirin box of record proportions. The box was produced by wrapping Bayer's corporate headquarters building in graphics. When the project was unveiled at the company's centennial celebration, the crowd of 45,000 people included 250 journalists from 29 countries and 17 television stations.

The graphics were output on a 5-m (16.4 ft) inkjet printer in 32 strips of a finely perforated, wind-permeable Ferrari PVC vinyl. The 5-m wide strips were installed by an athletic team of 30 "industrial mountaineers" who fearlessly scaled up and rappelled down the building.

To avoid drilling holes in the building, Makom's design team devised a graphics-support structure and steel crown capable of holding the more than 8.8 metric tons (9.7 tons) of vinyl graphics. Eight miles of straps, 7500 metal clips, 30,000 bolts, and 30,000 snap hooks were used to secure the graphics. Forty-eight air-filled tubes provided a cushion between the graphics and the office building's aluminum glass front and helped provide the box-like look. As each air-support tube was inflated, the strips of graphics were connected by 120-m (394-ft-long) zippers.

The wrap remained in place for two weeks, after which the 22,000-sq m (more than 236,000 sq ft) of vinyl graphics were cut into pieces and sewn into souvenir bags. *The Guinness Book of World Records* recognized the project as the "Largest Aspirin Pack in the World," and the largest inflatable structure. The zippers were also recognized as the longest ever produced.

M@kom®

PROJECT: Hotel Polonia Barricade Graphics, Warsaw, Poland
PRODUCTION: Makom/M. NUR, Kassel, Germany
PRINTING DEVICE: NUR Blueboard superwide inkjet printer

While the Hotel Polonia underwent a 22-month renovation project, Makom created a temporary facade that doubled as a new location for outdoor advertising. Makom enabled companies who wanted their messages seen by passersby on this well-traveled city street to buy and install graphics up to 52.5 x 19.2 m (172 ft x 63 ft) in this new space. Shown here is an advertisement for Vichy Laboratories that was posted for three months.

M@kom

PROJECT: Audi TT, Croatia
PRODUCTION: MetroMedia Technologies (MMT)
PRINTING DEVICE: MMT proprietary inkjet printing machines

One more example of a clean installation in a wallscape is this frontlit vinyl banner promoting the new Audi TT coupe. This advertising message measures 12 x 8 m, (39 ft x 26 ft), is installed using a clean-edge framing device, and accented with lights for night viewing.

PROJECT: Britney Spears Concert Promotion, Las Vegas, NV
PRODUCTION: Adera Corp., Las Vegas, NV, SkyTag Media, Beverly Hills, CA
PRINTING DEVICE: Vutek UltraVu 3360 superwide inkjet

Performers used to know they'd made it big when they saw their name in lights in Vegas or on Broadway. Now, superstars can measure their stature in the entertainment industry by the size of the graphics promoting their appearances. This 180 ft-high graphic of Britney Spears sporting an Elvis-like look appeared on the outside of the MGM Grand hotel to promote her concert special on HBO. SkyTag Media, a media company specializing in outdoor "spectaculars," coordinated the project and installation. Adera Corp. produced the graphics on Clear Focus SuperVue perforated window-graphics film.

PROJECT: Jerry Stackhouse Building Wrap, Southfield, MI
PRODUCTION: Northstar Imaging Solutions
PRINTING DEVICE: Vutek UltraVu 5300 superwide inkjet

To inspire civic pride and city-wide support for its NBA basketball team, the Detroit Pistons organization commissioned this 10-story building mural of one of its star players, Jerry Stackhouse. The adhesive-vinyl graphics, which called attention to the team's recent change in uniform colors, adorned the top floors of a 32-story office tower and could be seen from miles away. Northstar used a reflective graphic film from 3M Commercial Graphics that enabled the graphics to be seen at night.

PROJECT: Spider-Man Mural, Toronto, ON, Canada
PRODUCTION: ICON Digital Productions, Toronto, ON, Canada
PRINTING DEVICE: NUR Salsa superwide inkjet

A larger-than-life Spider-Man appears poised for action on the side of this building in Toronto's youthful and cosmopolitan College and Spadina neighborhood. To promote the premiere of the Sony Pictures' Spider-Man movie, Icon Digital Productions was hired to produce two 13.7- x 36.6-m (45- x 120-ft) banners for each side of the building. Output on 12-oz frontlit vinyl, the graphics were displayed in a building-mounted display system that enables large banners to be displayed wrinkle-free without a visible frame to detract from the impact of the visuals.

PROJECT: AIDS Ribbon on United Nations Building, New York, NY
PRODUCTION: Alkit Digital Imaging, New York, NY; Big Apple Visual Group, New York, NY

Not all wallscapes are used for commercial advertising. This 21-story window-mounted wrap on two sides of the United Nations Secretariat Building called attention to the first General Assembly special session on HIV/AIDS.
To make the AIDS Awareness Ribbon graphic visible at night, UN employees and volunteers followed a lights-on/lights-off plan devised by the building architect. Each night, they made sure that in designated offices, the blinds were closed and the lights were turned off. To illuminate the graphic, employees made sure that in other designated offices, the lights were left on and the blinds were left open.
The mural used about 40,000-sq ft (3716-sq m) of printed and cut adhesive-backed vinyl from Avery Dennison and other sources.

PROJECT: Kasimir project, Brussels, Belgium
PRODUCTION: MetroMedia Technologies (MMT)
PRINTING DEVICE: MMT proprietary inkjet printing machines

Belgian photo artist, Marin Kasimir, took pictures inside a four story office building, comprising different companies. Across from the office site, this sign was constructed to represent each floor of the office building from the inside-out. These four individual images each measure 2.16 x 21 m, and are printed frontlit vinyl material.

This photo-mural is a unique look at using large-format visuals to represent a theme without any advertising messages.

PROJECT: L'Oréal Paris Advertising, Budapest, Hungary
PRODUCTION: MetroMedia Technologies (MMT)
PRINTING DEVICE: MMT proprietary inkjet printing machines

To celebrate a management meeting of L'Oréal Worldwide in Budapest, a parking garage was covered with an open weave frontlit vinyl graphic. The images are vibrant during the day, and take on a glowing effect at night when front-positioned lights are turned on at dusk. This total image was comprised of four sections ranging in size from 18 x 17.35 m (59 x 67 ft) to 18 x 33.6 m (59 x 111 ft).

VEHICLE GRAPHICS

The term "promotional vehicle" has taken on a whole new meaning, now that it's possible to "wrap" cars, buses, boats, trailers, trains, trolleys, subway cars, airplanes, airport limos, and other vehicles in full-color, photographic-quality graphics.

A growing number of local and national businesses are using vehicle graphics to get more promotional mileage from their delivery trucks and bring ad messages to commuters, freeway travelers, and pedestrians in busy city centers.

Vehicles that drive predetermined routes in desirable neighborhoods and urban areas are being used as a medium for paid advertising, with movements tracked via satellites. Some ad-carrying vehicles travel to sites where crowds of people congregate. For instance, an ad-bearing truck may be driven around the block repeatedly or parked near a busy convention center, stadium, festival, or arena.

Vehicle graphics can either be adhered to the surface of the vehicle or carried in some sort of frame mounted on the vehicle. "Wraps" are created with thin, adhesive-backed vinyl films that conform to the curves of the vehicle. Starting from a template for the specific make and model of vehicle being wrapped, designers lay out the graphics in panels. The printed panels are applied to the vehicle by a trained installer, who knows how to align the panels, and make the vinyl stick smoothly, without gaps and wrinkles, even over corrugated trucksides or contoured bumpers.

Vehicle windows that look as if they are covered with opaque graphics are actually made with special one-way-see-through vinyl that allows occupants within the vehicle to see clearly out of the windows.

With premium-grade materials and adhesives, vehicle graphics can last up to five years or more and withstand the effects of airborne pollutants, rain, sunlight and repeated pressure washing. Less expensive materials that install quickly and remove cleanly make vehicle graphics viable for short-term promotions such as trade shows and events.

PROJECT: Hot Tamales Bus Wrap
PRODUCTION: Graphics System Installers Inc., Lakeland, FL;
The College Kit, Lebanon, NH
PRINTING DEVICE: Océ Arizona 180 large-format inkjet

Rock stars aren't the only ones who travel from city to city in specially outfitted buses. Brand marketers are using colorfully wrapped buses to take their products to where consumers are—at sporting events, outdoor festivals, and concerts.

The College Kit is an event-marketing company that helps brand marketers plan and coordinate such tours. The company is particularly proud of its skill in helping companies connect with college students in popular Spring Break destinations.

But buses aren't the only vehicles they take on the road. For a recent tour promoting Hot Tamales candy, designers from The College Kit teamed up with the production and installation pros from Graphic Systems Installers to create wraps for a Ford Taurus racing car, pickup truck, and 16- and 32-ft trailers. To ensure that the bold, attention-getting graphics wouldn't fade after several, rigorous months on the road, the pros at Graphics Systems Installers used Oracal's Orajet series 3691 white PVC film, 3M piezo inkjet series 3700 ink, and aN Oracal Oraguard series 210G laminate. The windows were wrapped with Clear Focus ClassicVue exterior-mount, one-way, see-through film.

The clean, smooth look of the graphics—even on grills and wheel wells—illustrates the value of relying on trained installers for vehicle graphic projects.

PROJECT: Nike SHOX Double-Decker Bus
PRODUCTION: Burton Imaging Group, Philadelphia, PA
PRINTING DEVICE: 3M Scotchprint Printer 2000 electrostatic system

When Nike rolled out its SHOX line of footwear, more than 200 graphics-wrapped busses also rolled out to deliver the message. The bus wraps—which were used as moving billboards—were generated by Burton Imaging Group, which specializes in all variations of transit and fleet advertising production.

PROJECT: UPS China Express
PRODUCTION: Deep Design, Atlanta, GA; Nite-Bright Signs, Ft. Myers, FL
PRINTING DEVICE: Scitex Idanit large-format inkjet

When UPS was cleared to make international deliveries to mainland China, the company decided to hold a press conference in front of the airplane that would be used when the new service was initiated. So the plane wouldn't look quite so plain, UPS turned to Deep Design Atlanta and Nite-Bright Signs to deliver a colorful, short-term graphic that could be installed and removed easily from the plane's side.
The 60-ft dragon graphics were inkjet-printed on Avery Dennison's Multi-Purpose Inkjet film, finished with a protective clearcoat, and applied to the 747 in time for the press conference. Due to federal flight regulations, the graphics were removed before the plane took off on its first flight to China.

PROJECT: New England Coffee Van Wrap, Malden, MA
PRODUCTION: Graphic Innovations and The RDW Group, Providence, RI
PRINTING DEVICE: Océ Arizona 180 large-format inkjet

New England Coffee is a third-generation family-owned business that prides itself on being one of the largest independent roasters in the field. This van, wrapped in 3M Scotchprint graphics, helps New England Coffee build awareness of its brand identity when the company brings coffee to community events such as the March of Dimes Walk, flower and garden shows, and the "World's Largest Pancake Breakfast." The pastoral graphics, designed by The RDW Group, are repeated on New England Coffee's website. The van-wrap graphics were produced by Graphic Innovations and installed by Hi-Image Fleet Graphics.

PROJECT: WBRU Radio Van Wrap, Providence, RI

PRODUCTION: Graphic Innovations and Logica Design, Providence, RI

PRINTING DEVICE: Océ Arizona 180 large-format inkjet

Whether traveling to a day-time promo or night-time concert, alternative rock station 95.5 WBRU makes its presence known with vehicle graphics that stand out in either the dark or the daylight. Graphic Innovations used 3M Scotchlite Reflective Graphic Film to create these 3M Scotchprint Graphics. The graphics were designed by Logica Design and installed by Hi-Image Fleet Graphics.

PROJECT: Experience Music Project, Seattle, WA
PRODUCTION: Supergraphics and McCann Erickson, Seattle, WA
PRINTING DEVICE: 3M Scotchprint Printer 2000 electrostatic system

To herald the opening of the Experience Music Project interactive music museum and IMAX Theatre, Supergraphics produced 3M Scotchprint graphics for the monorail that travels between Seattle's major tourist district and the Westlake Center shopping hub. Supergraphics also produced Scotchprint graphics for two articulated buses. The graphics theme, developed by the McCann Erickson agency, was repeated throughout Seattle's streets on 150 two-sided pole banners.

PROJECT: Chicago Trolley Wrap, Chicago, IL
PRODUCTION: Digital Printing Center, Chicago, IL
PRINTING DEVICE: Océ Arizona 180 large-format inkjet

The Chicago Trolley Company runs sightseeing trolleys on a 13-mile route through the heart of Chicago's hotel, shopping and entertainment districts. In addition to transporting tourists, the trolleys also now carry ad messages promoting current events and area attractions to Chicago residents as well as out-of-towners. The 3M Scotchprint Graphics are produced and installed by The Digital Printing Center in cooperation with designers from local and national ad agencies.

PROJECT: KOOL 93.1 FM Remote Trailer, Las Vegas, NV
PRODUCTION: Pictographics, Las Vegas, NV
PRINTING DEVICE: Vutek UltraVu 2360 large-format inkjet

The creative pros at radio station KOOL 93.1 came up with a cool idea for juicing up their remote-broadcast vehicle: Make an ordinary box trailer look like a beverage cooler! Pictographics printed the graphics on an Avery Dennison film with Easy Apply adhesive technology for fast installation. The graphics were finished with Avery Dennison overlaminate film for durability.

PROJECT: Airport Limo Van for Haier Electronics
PRODUCTION: Extreme Advertising & Promotion, New York, NY;
Burton Imaging, Philadelphia, PA
PRINTING DEVICE: 3M Scotchprint Printer 2000 electrostatic system

Companies can get some extra mileage from their investment in a
tradeshow by offering complimentary airport transportation to VIP
customers and prospects arriving for the show. Extreme Advertising &
Promotions wrapped this limo van to help Haier Electronics reinforce
its brand message when picking up customers arriving for a trade
show in Chicago.

The graphics were produced and installed by Burton Imaging
using 3M Controltac Plus changeable graphic film with Comply
adhesive technology for fast, wrinkle-free installation.

PROJECT: NFL/Campbell's Soup Promotion Caravan
PRODUCTION: Graphic Systems Installers, Lakeland, FL
PRINTING DEVICE: Xerox ColorgrafX electrostatic system

Before the National Football League and Campbell's Soup hit the road for a joint promotion, they decorated the fleet of vehicles to be used to transport personnel and supplies. The graphics combined Campbell's Chunky Soup branding images with images of Campbell's Soup spokesman Terrell Davis of the Denver Broncos. As part of the "Tackling Hunger" relief effort, which donated five million cans of soup to food banks nationwide, the colorful caravan traveled 25,000 miles. In various NFL cities and at the Super Bowl, road-trip personnel dispensed piping-hot samples of Chunky Soup to football fans who worked up an appetite playing "Chunky Challenge" inter-active games.

In addition to the graphics on the sides of the vehicles, graphics were applied to the tops of the bus and trailers for viewing by workers in high-rise office buildings in city centers and football fans on their way to the upper seats of each stadium.

The graphics were output on an Avery Dennison cast vinyl, and protected with a heavy-duty Teflon® overlaminate that could be easily cleaned if overzealous fans of Broncos' opponents spray-painted any messages of their own on the vehicles.

PROJECT: Beverage Promos on Vans and SUVs
PRODUCTION: PCL Graphics, Toronto, ON, Canada
PRINTING DEVICE: Vutek UltraVu 3360 superwide inkjet

Six- and 8-color, higher-resolution inkjet printers have made it easier to reproduce many of the customized corporate colors used in brand marketing. The digital-printing veterans at PCL Graphics are skilled in matching custom colors as evidenced by their work in these promotional vehicles for Powerade, Frappuccino, and Bacardi Silver.

PROJECT: Ad-Carrying Cars
PRODUCTION: FreeCar Media and Imagic, Los Angeles, CA
PRINTING DEVICE: Vutek UltraVu 2360 large-format inkjet printer and 3M Scotchprint Printer 2000 electrostatic system

Graphics-wrapped vehicles give advertisers a vibrant, cost-effective way to deliver ad messages to demographically targeted neighborhoods. FreeCar Media offers selected drivers the free use of a brand-new car or SUV for two years if they are willing to drive around with branding and ad messages such as the ones shown here for Tang, HBO's Oz series, and Jamba Juice. FreeCar also pays some drivers up to $400/month to allow their own vehicles to be wrapped for specified time periods.

To meet the requests of specific advertisers, drivers are selected on the basis of their lifestyles and driving patterns. To assure advertisers that the vehicles aren't simply parked in a garage somewhere, a satellite-based monitoring system verifies the location, speed, route and total mileage of each vehicle.

The vehicle graphics shown here were produced at Imagic, using a 3M graphic-marking film with Comply adhesive for fast, wrinkle-free installation. FreeCar's in-house art team provides design assistance to advertisers who want to take their messages to the streets.

PROJECT: Collateral Damage Hummer Wrap
PRODUCTION: PCL Graphics, Toronto, ON, Canada
PRINTING DEVICE: Vutek UltraVu 3360 superwide inkjet

To build awareness of the release of the Warner Brothers film *Collateral Damage*,
PCL Graphics accepted the mission to wrap this Hummer with promotional graphics.
Hummers tend to attract attention on any city street. But in this case, the rugged,
military-origin vehicle seems to mesh exceptionally well with the graphics for the
war movie starring Arnold Schwarzenegger.

PROJECT: The Daily Deal Sailboat
PRODUCTION: America's Cup Media, Sausalito, CA and Creatis Group, San Francisco, CA
PRINTING DEVICE: Superwide inkjet

Each day, thousands of people in San Francisco office buildings and high-rise hotels gaze out over the scenic San Francisco Bay. Dozens of sightseeing boats loaded with tourists also ply the Bay's waters. With this in mind, America's Cup Media gives advertisers an elegant new vehicle for "sails-manship" by providing 5000 sq ft of ad space aboard a retired America's Cup yacht.

For this project, which promoted the *Daily Deal* newspaper and website, the Creatis Group printed the yacht's sails on 7-oz vinyl. The company reinforce-stitched the seams to accommodate the breezy conditions on the Bay and produced complementary adhesive-vinyl graphics for the hull and boom.

America's Cup Media offers sailboat advertising programs in other major waterside cities, and invites key account executives and their clients to join them aboard the yacht as they sail the selected routes.

PROJECT: Mobile Backdrops for US Air Force Exhibits
PRODUCTION: Burton Imaging, Philadelphia, PA
PRINTING DEVICE: 3M Scotchprint Printer 2000 electrostatic system

The annual Ft. Lauderdale Air and Sea Show kicks off National Military Appreciation Month in May. An estimated 4 million spectators witness the series of events that the US military conducts in Ft. Lauderdale's skies and coastal waters.

To promote Air Force-related events at the show, Burton Imaging produced a series of 3M Scotchprint® vehicle wraps for show ground transportation and on city transit buses that carried out the same graphics theme used by the trucks carrying the US Air Force Experience traveling road show. The decorated vehicles provided a visual backdrop for a press conference and other Air Force events at the show.

PROJECT: Celebrate the Century Express Train
PRODUCTION: New Image Technologies, South Elgin, IL
PRINTING DEVICE: 3M Scotchprint Printer 2000 electrostatic system

As the turn of the millennium approached, the US Postal Service launched a commemorative stamp and education program honoring the most significant people, places, events and trends of the 20th Century. To support this "Celebrate-the-Century" program, the US Postal Service took this specially outfitted four-car Amtrak train to cities throughout the US. Equipped with interactive, multimedia exhibits, the train helped students and American history buffs travel back in time.

The train was decorated with 3M Scotchprint graphics produced and installed by New Image Technologies—a company whose owner has been installing vinyl graphics for more than 25 years. Against a parcel-like background, the design featured colorful enlargements of many of the 150 stamps from the Postal Services' "Celebrate-the-Century" series.

PROJECT: Ciena Limo
PRODUCTION: Burton Imaging, Philadelphia, PA
PRINTING DEVICE: 3M Scotchprint Printer 2000 electrostatic printer

Ciena, which makes optical networking systems, put a human face on its high-tech company with these 3M Scotchprint graphics applied to a limousine. Ciena officials used the limo to offer complimentary ground transportation to VIP customers and prospects attending a tradeshow at which Ciena was exhibiting.

PROJECT: Double-Decker Tour Bus Advertising, Chicago, IL
PRODUCTION: Digital Printing Center, Chicago, IL
PRINTING DEVICE: Océ Arizona 180 large-format inkjet

United Airlines and The Peggy Notebaert Nature Museum are two of the Chicago-area companies who have purchased advertising space on the sides of double-decker tour buses operated by the Chicago Double Decker Co.

During the buses' sightseeing tours through the heart of Chicago's hotel, shopping and entertainment districts, the ads are viewed by thousands of pedestrians, tourists, and bus passengers.

The 3M Scotchprint Graphics are produced and installed by The Digital Printing Center in cooperation with designers from local and national ad agencies.

PROJECT: Eddie Cheever Car in Disney 200
PRODUCTION: Freelance Lettering, Indianapolis, IN
PRINTING DEVICE: Gerber Edge thermal-transfer printer

How do you get racing-team business? Set up shop just a few miles from the track.
It also helps that Freelance Lettering owner Lance Gibbs has worked in the racing
industry for the past 30 years.

Most of the cut-to-shape decals, printed on Gerber adhesive vinyl films, are
applied at Gibb's shop or onsite at the track. Team Cheever, of Indianapolis,
designed the Eddie Cheever car around the sponsors' color schemes and logos, and
to fit the curves of the car.

PROJECT: Hollywood/Mercedes-Benz Truck Trailer
PRODUCTION: Freelance Lettering, Indianapolis, IN
PRINTING DEVICE: Gerber Edge thermal-transfer printer, 3M Scotchprint 2000 Printer electrostatic system

Besides race car logos and images, Freelance Lettering creates custom graphics for fuel trucks and show trailers. Pacwest Racing designed the "Hollywood graphic" to fully cover the oversized racing trailer. Adhesive-backed vinyl was applied to the trailer in 34-in. strips, similar to applying wallpaper. Upon completion, separate smaller decals were printed and cut to shape on the Gerber Edge, and applied to the front portion of the trailer and truck cab.

64 The Big Picture

RETAIL & POINT OF PURCHASE

Big visuals are used extensively in many retail environments. In addition to the short-term, P-O-P graphics used to call attention to items on sale, digitally printed, permanent graphics can be found decorating the walls, counters, columns, and windows. These permanent graphics are integral elements of the store's overall design and can help guide shoppers through a store or reinforce the retailers' brand identity.

Recent advances in display systems have made it possible to display graphics anywhere in the store and have empowered store personnel to easily change the graphics themselves. Other display technology improves the visual impact of printed graphics by adding the motion, depth, light and other special effects.

One advantage of using digitally printed graphics in retail settings is that the messages and images can be customized to appeal to various ethnic or demographic groups in different regions of the world. Graphics can also be output in different sizes to fit different size requirements at various branches. Larger stores often make space available to brand marketers who want to use big visuals to advertise specific products sold within.

Photo credit: Al Sypher, Image Associates, Plantation, FL

PROJECT: Dolphin Mall Signage, Miami, FL
PRODUCTION: Communication Arts, Boulder, CO; Sungraf Inc., Hallandale, FL
PRINTING DEVICE: NUR Salsa superwide inkjet

Although large-format digital printing technology is commonly used to produce, big, in-your-face visuals, digitally output prints aren't always the dominant graphic elements of architectural and wayfinding signs. Self-adhesive vinyls make it possible to apply graphic coverings to substrates of all types and sizes.

For the signage shown here, designers at Communications Arts used a combination of printed vinyls, 3D lettering and curved surfaces to create splashy, environmental signage that reflects Miami's rich, multicultural heritage.

The digital prints were supplied by Sungraf Inc., which used FLEXcon self-adhesive vinyls for most of the signs and 3M translucent white vinyl on the backlit lamppost signs. The signs were installed by Interstate Signcrafters of Boynton Beach, FL, and American Signcrafters of Bayshore, NY.

Project: Hyundai Backlit Advertising
PRODUCTION: MetroMedia Technologies (MMT)
Printing Device: MMT proprietary inkjet printing machines

This huge Hyundai car image was printed on opaque backlit material to produce a
brilliant, easy-to-view graphic both day and night, and from all sides. Fluorescent
bulbs on the inside of the framed lightbox provide illumination. Each panel for the top
of the three-sided sign measures 5.3 x 10.5 m (17 × 35 ft). The bottom text panels are
2.4 x 10.5 m (8 × 35 ft.).

PROJECT: Nutcracker Barbie Window Display at FAO Schwarz, New York, NY
PRODUCTION: Color by Pergament, New York, NY
PRINTING DEVICE: Vutek UltraVu 2360 large-format inkjet

Retailers can use short-term window graphics to add sparkle to their stores during the holiday season. These enchanting window graphics also helped promote Mattel's Nutcracker Barbie doll at the FAO Schwarz toy store. Printed on Avery Dennison's easily removable window-graphics film, the graphics were designed and produced to look as good to viewers inside the store as they did to people passing on the street.

PROJECT: XX XY Retail Graphics, Toronto, ON, Canada
PRODUCTION: Yabu Pushelberg; MetroMedia Technologies (MMT)
PRINTING DEVICE: MMT proprietary printing machines

Playing to the retail power of the Y-generation, Yabu Pushelberg designed this Canadian XX XY jeans/sportswear store to look and feel like a street store, balancing "urban-gritty" elements with a more refined look.

In the dramatic 50-ft wide x 30-ft high storefront, white neon "XX XY" letters float inside six-sided translucent acrylic suspended in front of translucent scrims. In a clever twist on words for retailer of fashion-forward jeans, the scrims feature a digitally printed mutating-genes pattern, using images of genes from biology textbooks. High sodium lights illuminate the scrims, helping give the storefront a glowing effect night or day. The scrim graphics were digitally printed by Metromedia Technologies.

The mutating genes theme is repeated on the selling floor, along with graphics identifying the store's target consumers—fashion-conscious 16- to 29- year olds.

PROJECT: Cleveland Browns Gridiron Square, Cleveland, OH
PRODUCTION: Retail Planning Associates, Columbus OH; AdMart International, Benton, KY; FastSigns, Cleveland, OH; Notre Monde, Columbus, OH
PRINTING DEVICE: Various wide-format and superwide inkjets

To draw crowds of fans to Cleveland Browns stadium even on non-game days, the Cleveland Browns organization developed the Gridiron Square area. This 12,000 sq ft space within the stadium combines The Browns Team Shop, The Grille and Sports Bar, and the Pepsi Cleveland Browns Hall of Fame Museum. Decorated in the team's signature orange and brown colors, the space features gargantuan graphics of some of Cleveland's most beloved Browns—including Paul Brown (for whom the team is named) and Hall-of-Fame running back Jim Brown. These images and four other well-known Browns players were selected from archival photographs, color-corrected and digitally printed on fireproof canvas. A UV-light-resistant coating was applied to prevent the images from fading. The canvas images are lashed to metal frames in a manner that alludes to the leather cord trussing on a football. Elsewhere, backlit images of current players are printed on clear acetate for quick changes.

PROJECT: GUESS? Staircase Graphics, San Francisco, CA
PRODUCTION: Andrés Imaging & Graphics, Chicago, IL
PRINTING DEVICES: Vutek 5300 superwide inkjet

Strong images demand buyers' attention in this staircase, which goes from street level to the second floor. These huge banners represent the sexy GUESS? look and provide color and image to the otherwise white painted walls. Printed on artist canvas, the texture enhances the flowing prints, and also allows for a nonglare finish for viewing indoors. These panels can also be seen from the street outside of the building, and may lure in shoppers.

PROJECT: Lazarus Beauty Spa, Columbus OH
PRODUCTION: Andrés Imaging & Graphics, Chicago, IL
PRINTING DEVICES: Vutek 3360 large-format inkjet

To represent a soft, latent image in this relaxing, pampered environment, a vinyl mesh fabric was employed and a feminine image chosen by the designer. The use of this type of environmental retail graphic can create mood and affect buying patterns.

The graphics were applied to retractable roller shades, and allow natural light to filter through.

PROJECT: Levi's Flagship, San Francisco, CA
PRODUCTION: Andrés Imaging & Graphics, Chicago, IL
PRINTING DEVICE: Xerox electrostatic system

To create a 3D look, these printed images were transferred onto prestained plywood via the dye-sublimation process. Using this process, applied heat and pressure turn the liquid toners into a gas, which permeates the surface for a total bond. The panels were then layered and overlapped to create the collage effect. This total graphic, designed by Jimmy Hornbeak, covered nearly an entire wall in the popular shopping spot.

This cash-out area was creatively designed to reinforce the Levi's SilverTab brand. Adhesive-coated rolled fencing material was stretched inside wood-trimmed alcoves with rubber "O" rings. The panels were lit front and back to create a rice-paper effect.

PROJECT: Tuscan Mural Artscape for Restaurant
PRODUCTION: DLM Studio, Cleveland, OH
PRINTING DEVICES: Vutek UltraVu 2360 large-format inkjet

Digitally printed wallcoverings provide a quick and easy way to enhance restaurant decor and ambience. This Mural Artscape, featuring a muted-tone, Tuscan Scenic motif, was designed by DLM Studio, which specializes in developing wallcoverings, fabrics and surface designs for the residential and commercial marketplace.

This Tuscan Scenic Mural Artscape is part of a collection of wallcovering murals that can be ordered in room-specific sizes through 4walls.com—an e-tailer of digitally printed wallcoverings and borders. 4walls.com also offers customizable murals and matching prints and decorative accessories.

PROJECT: DKNY Fragrance Launch Graphics, Bloomingdale's
PRODUCTION: Color X, New York, NY
PRINTING DEVICE: Proprietary system

Color X used digital printing on holographic paper, mounted on Gatorboard, for the launch of DKNY's new fragrance at Bloomingdale's. In all, 15,000 of the double-sided, 36- x 60-in. ethereal prints were produced for stores nationwide. Mounted images were scored and folded for worldwide shipping.

PROJECT: Cash Wrap in Soviet Jeans Store, Johannesburg, South Africa
PRODUCTION: Omnigraphics, Sandton, South Africa
PRINTING DEVICE: Vutek UltraVu 3300 superwide inkjet

Branding graphics posted at a store's checkout point are a good way to visually reinforce how merchandisers would like their stores to be perceived. Designers of this jeans store are cashing in on the versatility of the Fleximount II framing system, which holds vinyl graphics taut and wrinkle-free. Mounted nearly flush with the wall, the fast change-out display system makes it easy to keep fashion-forward graphics fresh.

PROJECT: CompUSA, San Francisco, CA
PRODUCTION: Andrés Imaging & Graphics, Chicago, IL
PRINTING DEVICES: Durst Lambda photo imager, Encad NovaJet Pro 850 large-format inkjet, Xerox ColorgrafX 8900 series electrostatic system

Brand consistency and recognition is shown here both inside and outside of this computer store. The location is on heavily traveled Market Street in downtown San Francisco, and the street-level window graphics capture attention from sidewalk and vehicle traffic. The 11 window graphics are made of backlit polyester material attached to the window mullions by springs and grommets. This installation provides for both a backlit and frontlit effect.

Take a look at the inside store graphics, and you'll see a media wall providing product info as well as directions to the store's basement selling floor. For in-your-face close-up graphics, a photo imager was chosen as the desired output device, providing crystal-clear photos without any dpi resolution detectable.

PROJECT: Storefront Façades at Roseville Galleria Mall, Roseville, CA
PRODUCTION: Ferrari Color Inc., Sacramento, CA
PRINTING DEVICE: Raster Graphics DCS electrostatic printing system

While these photos may look like actual storefronts, they are actually 3M Scotchprint graphics covering up the unsightly plywood barricades used while the BCBG and Coach stores were under construction. The stores weren't completed in time for the mall's grand opening, so the graphics gave mall shoppers a vivid, visual preview of what was "in store" in the near future. The graphics were designed by Urban Properties, the developer of the upscale Roseville Galleria Mall.

PROJECT: Aritzia, Toronto, ON, Canada
PRODUCTION: ICON Digital Productions, Toronto, ON, Canada
PRINTING DEVICE: 3M Scotchprint Printer 2000 electrostatic system

Aritzia, a clothing retailer targeting funky, individualistic young women, used window graphics to cover up the construction underway inside one of its new sites. The distinctive, brand-identity graphics enabled passersby to immediately recognize what store would be opening soon in the neighborhood.

PROJECT: Entryway Promotion at Hudson's Department Store, Toronto, ON, Canada

PRODUCTION: ICON Digital Productions, Toronto, ON, Canada

PRINTING DEVICE: 3M Scotchprint Printer 2000 electrostatic system

Department stores, such as Hudson's in downtown Toronto, are displaying graphics near busy entryways to help brand marketers add extra muscle to their ad campaigns. Digital printing technologies and quick-change display systems are making it more economically viable for retailers to display short-term advertising and seasonal messages. This attention-getting Scotchprint graphic for Ralph Lauren's Polo Sport fragrance was printed on 3M adhesive-backed vinyls and protected with a 3M overlaminating film.

PROJECT: Lowe's Home Decor Graphics
PRODUCTION: Pratt Screen and Digital Production, Indianapolis, IN
PRINTING DEVICES: NUR Blueboard superwide inkjet and Vutek UltraVu 2360 large-format inkjet

To support Lowe's goal to "Improve Home Improvement," Pratt Screen and Digital Production worked closely with Lowe's store-redesign team to develop a package of graphics that would improve the customer's shopping experience. After more than a year of collaboration, they accomplished their mission with this attractive blend of lifestyle imagery and logical, straightforward signage.

Pratt's design and engineering capabilities and production muscle in screen, digital and vinyl application, enabled Lowe's designers to proceed seamlessly from prototyping ideas through production and installation.

PROJECT: Wayfinding Graphics in Loblaws Store
PRODUCTION: PCL Graphics, Toronto, ON, Canada
PRINTING DEVICE: Vutek UltraVu 3360 superwide inkjet

Big, colorful visuals can not only reinforce a store's branding, but also help shoppers quickly distinguish one section of a big store from another. The permanent graphics shown here are part of the interior design of Loblaws grocery stores. The graphics were printed on a 4-mil calendered, adhesive-backed vinyl from Avery Dennison.

PROJECT: Urban Stage Entertainment Court at Concord Mills, Charlotte, NC

PRODUCTION: Kiku Obata & Co., St. Louis, MO; Microlens Technology, Matthews, NC; Transistor 6, Oakland, CA; Mega media Concepts Ltd., Springfield, VA; Sign Art, Charlotte, NC

PRINTING DEVICES: Various inkjets

Concord Mills is a destination retail/entertainment complex featuring more than 200 stores, a 24-screen movie theater, themed restaurants and a festive food court. The center's design incorporates regional imagery, celebrating North Carolinians' love of music, crafts, auto racing, basketball, fashion, gardens and urban life.

This Urban Stage Entertainment Court is designed to communicate the energy and attitude of a great city. Designers commissioned graffiti artists to create a mural depicting nightlife, jazz clubs, dining out and city fun. The forever fresh and changing nature of urban life is conveyed in a steel framework that combines tri-vision and lenticular panels displaying a changing assortment of colorful, layered and abstract images. The display area also includes digital images printed on mesh, aluminum and transparent screens.

PROJECT: AMC 30 Theater Complex at the Block, Orange, CA
PRODUCTION: Murphy and Co., Los Angeles, CA; Gordon Sign, Denver, CO
PRINTING DEVICE: Scitex Idanit large-format inkjet

Just as digital audio has enhanced the moviegoing experience with ear-opening surround-sound, digital imaging and printing technology makes it possible to surround moviegoers in eye-opening images.

To make this 30-screen AMC theatre complex stand out, the urban-planning and architecture firm Jerde Partnership International used larger-than-life imagery of some of cinema's biggest stars to thematically recreate some of the glitz and glamour of Hollywood through the years. Jerde hired Murphy and Co. to serve as lead graphic designers for the visuals.

The design team divided the project into three "visitor experiences": approaching the multiplex, buying a ticket, and seeking a specific auditorium.

People approaching the theater are guided by softly colored, backlit graphics that line the entranceway, creating a lantern-like effect. Upon entering the lobby rotunda, moviegoers walk onto a terrazzo floor decorated with quotes from popular films. Looking up, they get a clearer view of the 20- × 150-ft semi-circular cyclorama that they first glimpsed from afar through a glass wall as they approached the theater.

To keep the cyclorama from becoming dated, the mural was created in layers, with historical cinema images in the background. Protruding 4 or 8 in. from the background layer are smaller, framed graphic panels featuring more contemporary movie scenes. These panels can be easily updated with fresh images.

Once moviegoers buy their tickets, they wander down image-lined corridors to the auditorium showing their chosen film.

Through the magic of modern digital-imaging software, graphic designers added some visual flair to familiar images, by recreating them with either a painterly or stylized look.

The images were output at Gordon Sign on a 4-mil calendered vinyl and finished with a matte, protective clearcoat.

The Day of the Dead celebrates the cycle of life and death by remembering dead ancestors. Chicanos reinvented this traditional Mexican holiday as a means of artistic and cultural expression, often celebrating it in public places like neighborhood stores, cultural centers, and museums.

Celebración de la Vida y la Muerte

El Día de los Muertos celebra el ciclo de la vida y la muerte recordando a los antepasados fallecidos. Los chicanos reinventaron esta celebración mexicana tradicional como un medio de expresión artística y cultural, celebrándola a menudo en lugares públicos tales como las tiendas del barrio, los centros culturales y los museos.

"When you have the concept that there is no difference between life and death and that it is all part of this natural cycle, then you can believe in going back and forth."
—Tere Romo, art curator

"Cuando tienes la idea de que no hay diferencia entre la vida y la muerte y que todo es parte de este ciclo natural, puedes creer en ir y venir."
—Tere Romo, curadora de arte

eich
ENSKUNST

90 The Big Picture

BUILDS

RSA Conference
RSA CONFERENCE 2

MUSEUM & EXHIBITION GRAPHICS

At museums and exhibitions, digitally printed
graphics guide visitors, promote corporate
sponsors, provide visual backdrops for events
and displays, and explain the exhibit being viewed.

In order to withstand the closer scrutiny and
frequent touching by the visiting public, graphics
created for museum settings frequently require
high-resolution output methods and fingerprint-
resistant, glare-free finishing techniques.

PROJECT: RSA Security Conference 2001, San Francisco ,CA
PRODUCTION: GES Exposition Services, San Francisco, CA; ABI Airbrush Images, Conroe, TX; Giant Impressions, Santa Clara, CA; Adera Corp., Las Vegas, NV
PRINTING DEVICE: Vutek UltraVu 5300 superwide inkjet, Encad NovaJet 500 inkjet; 3M Scotchprint 2000 electrostatic system

As competition for trade-show attendees has intensified, trade-show management teams have taken steps to enhance the attendees' on-site experiences. Large-format graphics can help create discernible differences among trade shows in the minds of attendees.

When the RSA Security Conference was held at the Moscone Center for the first time, GES Exposition Services' design team met with the show-management company, LKE Productions, to come up with an action plan.

To add a high-tech feel to this conference on internet cryptology and security issues, they decided to develop a package of science-themed graphics. They chose artwork supplied by CODA Creative of Oakland, CA, referencing the deep-space voyage of the Pioneer 10 spacecraft.

Taking advantage of Moscone's spacious architecture, GES' lead designer for the project used every opportunity to blast the artwork big. The two largest treatments involved wrapping the exterior of the North Hall with images printed on Clear Focus perforated vinyl window-graphics film and producing a 16- x 60-ft seamless, backlit banner in the lower lobby. The window graphics drew visitors to the proper building entrance, and the glowing, backlit wall kept the energy rising. To imprint the theme, related graphics in various sizes and formats were used throughout the event areas.

Another distinguishing characteristic was the treatment of sponsorship graphics. Show-management companies typically sell ad space in lobbies, registration areas, and entrances so exhibitors can entice attendees to their booths. To avoid the risk of clashing graphics, show producers agreed to keep public-area graphics in the show theme and provide spots for sponsor logos to integrate with the look. A variety of sponsorship opportunities were offered, such as custom columns, stair graphics, banners, kiosks, and laminated countertops in food-service areas.

Because RSA Conference attendees were new to Moscone, show producers considered wayfinding signage critical. The same bold colors and theme used throughout the show were repeated on wayfinding signage. This also helped keep RSA Conference attendees from getting mixed up with attendees of concurrent shows who were traveling some of the same corridors and lobbies.

The window graphics on the North Hall of Moscone were produced by Adera Corp.

PROJECT: Museum of Science and Industry, Chicago, IL
PRODUCTION: AK Flag and Banner, Little Rock, AR
PRINTING DEVICE: Vutek UltraVu 5000 superwide inkjet

Banners placed at this museum across from Lake Michigan in downtown Chicago, are perfect illustrations of how "The Windy City" got its nickname. To take some stress off the hanging system, these 9.5- x 29-ft banners were printed on mesh material. Special rigging devices designed by Sterling Sails, ensured quick change-out by using ropes and pulleys.

The porticos in front of the museum make a great stage for all types of graphics, including individual vignette images or a large bannerscape.

PROJECT: Children's Own Museum, Toronto, ON, Canada
PRODUCTION: ICON Digital Productions
PRINTING DEVICE: NUR Salsa large-format inkjet, Xerox ColorgrafX 8954 electrostatic system

This isn't your ordinary museum…it's designed specifically for children with the intent of making learning fun, and hands on. Part of this lively ambience is conveyed by the bright orange and yellow graphics found inside and out, on signs of all sizes.

To keep the graphics and interactive exhibits sticky-finger proof, a matte overlaminate was applied. Laminating also increases the durability of signage, and is washable and scrubbable.

PROJECT: Just Born Candy Company Trade-show Exhibit
PRODUCTION: onPoint Visuals, Boston, MA; Inova Exhibit Projects, Mt. Laurel, NJ
PRINTING DEVICE: Raster Graphics DCS 5442 electrostatic printer and
Astechnologies' Astex heat-transfer press

Mike and Ike and Hot Tamales candies are familiar products, but few people realize
that Just Born, Inc. is the company that makes them. Inova Exhibit Projects helped
Just Born address this problem by designing a trade-show booth that seamlessly
combined rigid, corporate-looking Just Born identity graphics with digitally imaged,
lightweight fabrics that replicated its colorful package graphics. The super-sized
candy boxes at the top of each column were created from fabrics stretched over
aluminum framing systems.

   To print the fabrics, onPoint Visuals used the dye-sublimation process, which
permanently fuses the toners to the fabrics for a natural feel and greater durability.

PROJECT: Kellogg's Reconfigurable Trade-show Exhibit
PRODUCTION: iG3 Integrated Graphics, Concord, ON, Canada; Geron Associates, Markham, ON, Canada
PRINTING DEVICE: Scitex Vision Grandjet V5 superwide inkjet

Geron Associates designed this multiconfigurable trade-show exhibit for Kellogg's Canada. With tower and fascia shapes suggesting a cereal box and bowl, the booth integrates Kellogg's red and white corporate-identity colors with product colors such as Raisin Bran purple and Rice Krispies blue.

   Built in 8-ft high sections, each 20 x 20 ft. module can break down into a 10 x 10 or 10 x 20 ft. display. Or, two display modules can be aligned for a 10 x 40 ft booth space. The graphics were printed on a 19 oz. backlit material from Seemee Verseidag, then installed in iG3's Fleximount II, low-profile, adjustable, graphics-tensioning system. The Fleximount II system gives the graphics a frameless, clean look while enabling them to be moved from one podium to another as needed and transported without creases.

Photo credit: Heather Watson, designer

PROJECT: Chicano Now Exhibit
PRODUCTION: Hunt Design Associates, Pasadena, CA; Wyatt Design Group Inc., Pasadena, CA; Williams Graphics, Sylmar, CA
PRINTING DEVICE: Roland Hi-Fi JET high-resolution inkjet

For Clear Channel Entertainment-Exhibitions, the Wyatt Design Group prepared a 5000-sq ft traveling exhibit to explain the rich contributions Chicanos have made to American society. Shown here at the Alameda Museo Americano in San Antonio, TX, the Chicano Now exhibit was produced in collaboration with actor and art collector Cheech Marin and features custom, original art, three-dimensional environments, artifacts, film/video presentations, music, and original performances.

To convey the content of the exhibit, Wyatt Design Group hired Hunt Design Associates to create a series of bold, but not overpowering, graphic panels. Hunt followed through with brightly colored, informative, inspiring graphics that suggest the multilayered Chicano heritage. The panels were balanced with both English and Spanish text.

William Graphics printed Hunt's designs on 4-mil, pressure-sensitive vinyl, which was mounted, then overlaminated with a satin-finish Lexan for durability. All panels were computer cut to size and shape.

PROJECT: Altoona Railroader's Museum, Altoona, PA
PRODUCTION: E.B. Luce Corp., Worcester, MA; Christopher Chadbourne and Assoc., Cambridge, MA; Sparks Exhibits & Environments, Philadelphia, PA
PRINTING DEVICE: Océ Lightjet 5000 photo imager, Colorspan high-resolution inkjet

Over 600 images, a variety of materials, and special coloring techniques were used to create this "hand-colored" effect. The challenge was to bring together all the different media to achieve a uniform appearance. Wrapped edges and seams created a clean look, and enhanced the durability of the graphics, which are printed on Ilford's Ilfocolor photo paper and inkjet media.

PROJECT: Interior Glass-Wall Graphics at Copia, Napa, CA
PRODUCTION: Supergraphics, Seattle, WA; West Office Exhibition Design, Oakland, CA
PRINTING DEVICE: 3M Scotchprint Printer 2000 electro-static system

Full-wall window graphics of a kitchen, dining room, and wine cellar provide a creative interior-design solution for three glass-walled rooms that are part of the "Forks in the Road" permanent exhibit at Copia: The American Center for Wine, Food & The Arts.

The graphics draw attention to the center of each room, which feature presentations on how culinary traditions from around the world have been integrated into other traditions in the US. From the main exhibit area, visitors can see into each room. But once inside each room, all they see are the surrounding wall graphics.

The window-wall graphics were designed by West Office Exhibition Design of Oakland, CA, and printed by SuperGraphics' San Jose, CA division, using Clear Focus Imaging's ClassicVUE perforated, vinyl film.

PROJECT: Minnesota Zoo Tiger Lair
PRODUCTION: Science Museum of Minnesota
PRINTING DEVICE: HP Designjet 5000 inkjet

When the Science Museum of Minnesota moved into a brand-new facility, an in-house graphics production center was born. The shop now exists as a separate profit center and provides graphics for other nonprofit entities, such as the Minnesota Zoo. After printing, these images were embedded into a solid plastic composite to survive extreme temperatures and climate changes.

PROJECT: San Diego Hall of Champions, San Diego, CA
PRODUCTION: Pictographics, Las Vegas, NV
PRINTING DEVICE: Vutek UltraVu 2360 inkjet, MacDermid Colorspan hi-res inkjet, Raster Graphics 5442 electrostatic system

Created as a tribute to San Diego's homegrown champions, the Hall of Champions is housed in a renovated building in Balboa Park and includes a variety of displays and exhibits that incorporate various digital and traditional signs and displays. Graphics were printed or applied to banner vinyls, fabrics, flexface materials, and even super-sticky and durable floor-graphic substrates. Built to be more than a museum and archive of San Diego sports, 70,000-sq ft facility is three levels and has hands-on exhibits and interactive displays.

PROJECT: "The Streak, Cal Ripken, Baseball's Ironman,"
Babe Ruth Museum, Baltimore, MD
PRODUCTION: Adler Display, Inc., Visual Impressions
PRINTING DEVICE: 3M Scotchprint Printer 2000 electrostatic
system

The Babe Ruth Museum in Baltimore commissioned this timeline
of Cal Ripken's record-breaking streak of 3,000 consecutive
baseball games played. The mural also depicts Lou Gehrig,
whose record Ripken eclipsed. For high detail and close viewing,
graphics like these require quality digital output, and color
consistency obtained by using the high-resolution printing
option on the 3M Scotchprint 2000 system.

PROJECT: Decorative Wall at Design Conference in Austria
PRODUCTION: Typico Megaprints GmbH and Co.
PRINTING DEVICE: Proprietary superwide airbrush

To create a dramatic, temporary wall structure for a design expo in Austria, Typico Megaprints used its proprietary computer airbrush printer to decorate 6600 sq ft of Ferrari vinyl mesh, which was stretched wrinkle-free over the support structure.

Photo credit: Walter Klocker

PROJECT: Giorgetti Salone del Mobile, Milan, Italy
PRODUCTION: eXtraLarge Italia, division of the Vertical Vision Group
PRINTING DEVICE: NUR Blueboard superwide inkjet

Positive-negative images in bright contrasting colors enliven this
trade-show booth for an Italian furniture manufacturer.

ENVIRONMENTS

Digitally printed visuals are adding personality and appeal to gathering places such as restaurants, waiting areas, theaters, and corporate lobbies. For special events, graphics are being used to totally transform an environment built for one purpose into a setting more suited for a different purpose.

Some designers choose to bring color and vibrancy to otherwise plain surfaces; others use soft and muted colors to create a relaxing ambience for diners. Corporations are using environmental graphics to make a visual statement about the company's history and links to the community. Many of these messages are conveyed via digitally reproduced archived photos, art reproductions, or logo patterns.

PROJECT: Eureka Waterfront Kiosks, Eureka, CA
PRODUCTION: Agreda Communications, Cutten, CA
PRINTING DEVICE: HP Designjet 2500CP Inkjet

These kiosks are part of a Northern California costal town's Waterfront Boardwalk. To contend with the Eureka's rainy, damp weather, as well as the sunny days, LexJet's inkjet vinyl and UV-resistant overlaminate solution were chosen.

PROJECT: Galaxy Theater at the Telluride Film Festival, Telluride, CO
PRODUCTION: Telluride Film Festival Production Crew
PRINTING DEVICE: Roland Hi-Fi JET Pro and CAMMJet high-resolution inkjets

Every Labor Day weekend, film buffs and Hollywood movers and shakers gather for the Telluride Film Festival. For the four-day event, school cafeterias and gymnasiums throughout the quaint, mountain town are magically transformed into themed movie theaters.

For example, for most of the year, the 490-seat Galaxy Theater shown here is actually the gymnasium of the Telluride Elementary School. Telluride Film Festival art director Garry Transue spearheaded the transformation, choosing graphics that showed how the future was envisioned by forward thinkers of the 16th and 17th centuries. Some of the images used were reproductions of engravings, while others were created new to fit the theme. Independent artist Transue completed a lot of the design work in his studio in Sonoma, CA. Then, as the Festival's opening drew closer, he worked with the on-site Telluride Film Festival Production Crew to produce and install the interior and exterior graphics that help turn a gym into a theater. One of the key design challenges is to produce artwork that is easy to install and store. All the elements are packed away into semi-trailer trucks for storage from year to year.

The Galaxy Theater project featured more than 20 inkjet-printed graphics—the largest measuring 12 by 17 ft. Other elements supporting the Galaxy Theater's theme were a sculpture garden, columns of light, and a video projected on screen as the audience files in.

Other Telluride Film Festival theaters that Transue helped developed include the Chuck Jones cinema, which pays homage to the animator who created Bugs Bunny and other Looney Tunes characters, and an Egyptian art-deco themed movie palace.

PROJECT: Maryland Aviation and Space History, BWI Airport, Baltimore, MD
PRODUCTION: Adler Display, Baltimore, MD, Visual Impressions, Charlotte, NC
PRINTING DEVICE: 3M Scotchprint Printer 2000 electrostatic system

This exhibit in the Baltimore-Washington International Airport was designed to convey the story of Maryland's contribution to space and aviation exploration. The mural measures 175 ft x 28 ft (53.4 x 8.5 m), and contains 25 different panels overlaying the background graphics that depict certain events or contributions.

PROJECT: I-95 Maryland Welcome Center, Calverton, MD

PRODUCTION: Adler Display, Baltimore, MD; Visual Impressions, Charlotte, NC; Optima Graphics, Fenton, MO

PRINTING DEVICE: 3M Scotchprint Printer 2000 electrostatic system, Durst Lambda photo imager

Visitors to this I-95 Welcome Center in Maryland stop to get information on the state's most popular destinations. A 90-ft long mural that wraps around the walls of the Center, depicts what awaits them in every direction. The graphics are applied to the walls in the actual direction they are located. For example, western ski resorts appear on a west-facing wall, Washington, DC appears on a south facing wall, etc. The murals were output as 3M Scotchprint graphics, while backlit graphics were imaged by Optima Graphics using a Durst Lambda for true photographic quality.

PROJECT: Cereal Adventure, Mall of America, Bloomington, MN
PRODUCTION: Vomela Specialties Co., St. Paul, MN; New Image Technologies, South Elgin, IL; Shea Architects Inc., Minneapolis, MN
PRINTING DEVICE: 3M Scotchprint Printer 2000 electrostatic system, HP Designjet 5000 inkjet

An environment geared towards children needs graphics to be two things: durable and cleanable. The rainbow of colorful graphics meets these criteria and provides a third visual interest.

One of the project's biggest challenges was installation constraints and timing. New Image Technologies had to install the graphics after hours, between 10 p.m. and 7 a.m. to avoid shopper interruption.

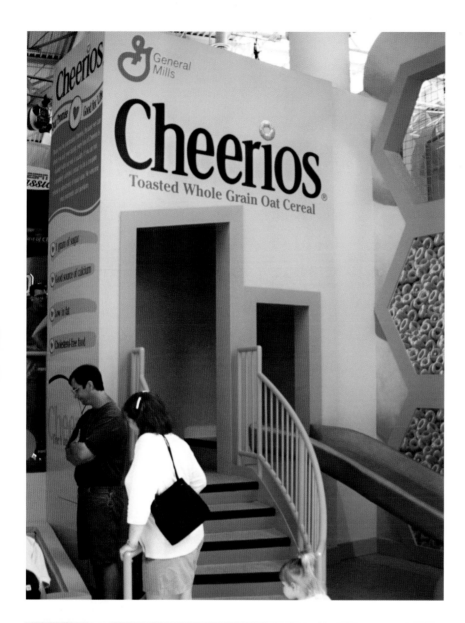

PROJECT: Scotchprint® Graphics Safari, San Francisco, CA
PRODUCTION: Mega Arts, Transportation Displays, Inc.
PRINTING DEVICE: 3M's Scotchprint Printer 2000 electrostatic system, Vutek UltraVu 5300 superwide inkjet, Scitex Pressjet-W inkjet and Océ Arizona inkjet

For several weeks, San Francisco train commuters encountered vibrant-colored photo realistic jungle scenes that covered walls, pillars, floors and trash cans throughout Powell Street Station. 3M transformed the station to demonstrate how users can put their brands on unique surfaces like never before with Scotchprint graphics.

Nearly 6,000 sq ft of 3M Scotchprint graphics, including extra large floor graphics depicting fern leaves, 900 6-in. green tree frogs, multiple 7-ft tigers, King Kong-sized monkeys and brightly-colored toucans, were used.

Materials included 3M's Floor Graphic film 8660, Scotchprint Graphics for sidewalk signs Overlaminate 8947, Scotchprint Floor Graphic Overlaminate Clear film 8945, Scotchcal Graphic film 3630-20 and 8643, Blackline Screen film, Controltac Plus Graphic film 180C and 180-10C with Comply Performance and Scotchcal clear graphic film 3500-114.

PROJECT: Virgin Active Health Gyms, Sandton, South Africa
PRODUCTION: Omnigraphics, Sandton, South Africa
PRINTING DEVICE: Vutek UltraVu 3300 superwide inkjet

These brilliant graphics bring an inspiring sense of energy to the pool area of a health club. The graphics, printed on sign fabrics from Verseidag Seemee, are tensioned in a slender-profile Fleximount II framing system, that makes it possible to create easily changeable wall murals in a variety of dimensions.

PROJECT: Residential Murals, Atlanta, GA
PRODUCTION: Totally Custom Wallpaper, Atlanta, GA
PRINTING DEVICE: Raster Graphics DCS electrostatic printing system

Custom-designed wallcovering murals can help homeowners design living spaces that reflect their personalities and interests. When Bill and Bev Plummer were planning their dream home in an Atlanta suburb, they decided to spice up the decor with art-inspired wallcovering murals. To surround guests in a downstairs recreational area with the joyful spirit of Parisian life, they hired Totally Custom Wallpaper to digitally reproduce the impressionist painting *Le Moulin de la Galette*, by Pierre-Auguste Renoir. The mural was applied to a concave wall opposite a mirror.

To create the illusion of spectators in a recreational boxing area, the Plummers ordered a wallcovering mural made from a digital reproduction of the painting *Dempsey & Firpo* by realist George Bellows.

For both murals, Totally Custom Wallpaper used an electrostatic transfer printing process and a latex-saturated paper stock from InteliCoat. The latex-based media has the thickness of traditional wallcoverings, making it possible to hide imperfections in the walls being covered. Unlike adhesive-vinyl murals that require specially trained installers, wallcovering murals created with latex-saturated papers can be installed by conventional, professional wallpaper hangers.

Totally Custom Wallpaper also markets customized wallpaper borders, fabrics, ceramic tiles, and cabinetry.

PROJECT: Computer Associates Headquarters Atrium, Islandia, NY
PRODUCTION: Display Presentations Ltd., onPoint Visuals
PRINTING DEVICE: Vutek 5300 superwide inkjet

The 60-ft atrium spans the entire height of this six-story building. To enhance the environment, Display Presentations Ltd. printed these graphics on Celtic cloth, and onPoint Visuals was called upon to manufacture the hanging elements using tension fabric for the circles, and stretched spandex mesh for the flat panels.

PROJECT: Custom Wallcoverings for 4Walls.com
PRODUCTION: DLM Studio, Cleveland, OH
PRINTING DEVICES: Vutek UltraVu 2360 large-format inkjet and Xeikon digital press

Designers in retail, residential and institutional settings can use digitally printed wallcoverings to add flair and style to otherwise plain spaces. Colors can be tweaked to match flooring and furniture or existing design elements. Murals can be sized to fit existing spaces. And panoramic, mural-style borders can extend well beyond the 20- to 24-in. lengths of small, repeating patterns found on conventional wallpaper borders.

One firm specializing in digitally imaged wallcoverings is 4walls.com, an e-tailer of assorted Mural ArtScapes and customizable murals and mural-style borders for waiting rooms, lobbies, children's rooms, restaurants, stores, and other environments. The company also sells matching accessories, including digitally printed blinds, prints, and cut-outs.

The graphics on pages 122-125 were designed by DLM Studio, which specializes in developing wallcoverings, fabrics and surface designs for the residential and commercial marketplace.

PROJECT: impact Mural in Redwood Tower Lobby, Baltimore, MD
PRODUCTION: Visual Impressions, Charlotte, NC; Adler Display, Inc., Baltimore, MD
PRINTING DEVICE: 3M Scotchprint Printer 2000 electrostatic system

This decorative, impact mural enhances the look and feel of the lobby of the Redwood Tower office building in Baltimore. Designed by Adler Displays, the mural uses a collage of images output as 3M Scotchprint® graphics to help bring the Baltimore cityscape into the office tower.

PROJECT: Diploma Mural, Long Island University, Brooklyn, NY
PRODUCTION: Power Graphics, Salt Lake City, UT; Richard Pasquarelli, New York, NY
PRINTING DEVICE: Hewlett-Packard Designjet 5000UV high-resolution inkjet

Artist Richard Pasquarelli created this 3 x 65 ft mural entitled Diploma for a curved wall in the lobby of the Salena Gallery on the Brooklyn campus of Long Island University. Pasquarelli used his own memories of college life to create a collage of images, then sent the file to printmakers he trusted at Power Graphics.

Power Graphics output the mural in three sections on Magic® wet-strength paper, then applied an adhesive backing. The mural was installed by Pasquarelli, his wife, and friends.

PROJECT: Hometown Heroes, Toronto, ON, Canada
PRODUCTION: ICON Digital Productions, Toronto, ON, Canada
PRINTING DEVICE: Vutek 3360 superwide inkjet

Graphics were produced for the inside and outside of Toronto's SkyDome to celebrate the legends and careers of Toronto's local baseball heroes, and to mark the 25th anniversary of the team. Shown here are 3M Scotchprint graphics that were designed and output with a ghosting effect so they weren't a distraction to players on the inside stadium walls. Also shown are banners that were output onto Neschen's TCS flag material for display around the perimeter of the stadium. 3M Scotchprint Graphics for Sidewalk Signs were also used along some of the concrete walls of the SkyDome, as well as on the tops of the dugouts and in the bullpen. The project finished at installing nearly 10,000 sq ft (929 sq m) of vinyl graphics.

PROJECT: Ticket Center Graphics at The Breakers, Newport, RI
PRODUCTION: Graphic Innovations, Providence, RI; Fleming & Roskelly Inc., Newport, RI
PRINTING DEVICE: Hewlett Packard Designjet 5000 inkjet

The Breakers, a 70-room villa built for Cornelius Vanderbilt II, is the grandest of Newport's summer "cottages" and a symbol of the Vanderbilt family's pre-eminence in the late 19th century. Preserved as a national historic landmark, the Italian Renaissance-style house is open for tours.

Visitors standing in line to buy tour tickets can learn more about The Breakers by viewing a series of thirty-five 5- x 5-ft prints designed by Fleming & Roskelly, Inc. Displayed on a deck beneath a tent roof, the Sintra®-mounted prints also function as walls. To withstand the rigors of outdoor exposure, Graphic Innovations output the prints on an adhesive-backed vinyl from Ilford Imaging and protected them with a UV-light-resistant Ilford overlaminate film.

DIGITAL FINE ART

The term "digital fine art" is used in two different ways: 1) To describe a work of art created on a computer; and 2) To refer to hand-drawn or hand-painted works of art that have been digitally reproduced.

The rise of digital printmaking has made it economically feasible for artists at all stages of their careers to produce limited editions of their works. Instead of producing and storing hundreds of copies of their artwork, artists can now create a digital master, and then reproduce copies as they are purchased. The art can be proofed and/or reproduced in a variety of sizes, on a variety of substrates ranging from canvas and watercolor papers to T-shirts, coffee mugs, and mousepads.

PROJECTS: Silver Maple Gallery Exhibit
ARTIST: Barry Stein
OUTPUT DEVICE: Epson Stylus Pro 1270 inkjet

"Walking through the narrow passages and back alleys of an ancient city such as Venice or Sarlat, I bathe my senses in the soft textures and time-worn patterns of countless individuals, imprints. These experiences are the beginning of the process by which my images are created," says artist Barry Stein. *Bench Hands*, Tavira, Portugal, shows some of the older men who congregate every afternoon throughout Spain and Portugal on benches in the center of town to talk and relax. *Covered Passage*, Lyon, France, uses soft pastel colors on the masonry to accent the hidden passages and spiral stairways built for the silk trade and later used by the French Resistance in WWII. *Des Recollets*, Sarlat, France, shows the back alleys of Sarlat with their medieval ambiance that ignites imagination of life in an ancient walled city where children still play today. *Eternal Beauty*, Paris, France, depicts an ancient Mesopotamian vision of beauty brought to life.

PROJECT: Sound Waves
ARTIST: Karin Schminke
PRINTING DEVICE: Epson Stylus Pro 9500 inkjet

This project was created as a permanent installation for the University of Washington Bothell and Cascadia Community College's new campus. Because the campus includes 58 acres of restored wetlands, the artist chose lenticular technology for its ability to capture movement and depth—and to mimic light dancing on water like viewing tidal pools. The installation consists of five 36-in. panels printed on white vinyl film and finished with MicroLens 20-line lenticular lenses.

PROJECTS: Various Titles
ARTIST: Myra Mandel
PRINTING DEVICES: Roland CAMMJET CJ500 inkjet/cutter,
ColorSpan Display Maker Mach XII inkjet

Israeli artist Myra Mandel incorporates two sources of inspiration into her art: shapes and textures from nature, and the poetry of the bible. Through a combination of traditional acrylic painting and digital technologies, Mandel uses photo editing and painting software to compose images that include Hebrew text and then prints them onto various weights and textures of canvas. One technique the artist employs is selecting random bits of images and pasting them on top of other images with partial opacity. She also uses special effects with much of the Hebrew biblical text in her work, making the text look rough and half-erased as letters carved in stone or eroded by time would be.

PROJECT: Passing the Ball
ARTIST: Ina Gilbert
PRINTING DEVICE: Epson Stylus Pro 9000 inkjet

This is one of a related series of digitally created paintings by the artist. It will be printed in an edition of up to six "original" prints, on paper and canvas in various sizes. She says it portrays the profiles of two talking heads emerging from a shared oval contour, suggesting both a connection and motion. The head on the right is shouting, while the one on the left is about to interrupt. The conversational ball is about to move.

PROJECT: My Kansas City
ARTIST: Charlie Roberts
PRINTING DEVICE: Encad NovaJet 700 inkjet

High school student Charlie Roberts, a Kansas native, was introduced to digital fine-art printmaking when he was contacted to participate in a case study for *The Big Picture* magazine. His original art was created on newsprint with pen-and-ink and oil paint. Digital reproduction allowed the artist to intensify the colors, and create multiple sizes of the original work on a variety of art papers. Shown here is one of the artist's proofs which remains in a private collection. His first print run sold out completely, and a second edition is forthcoming.

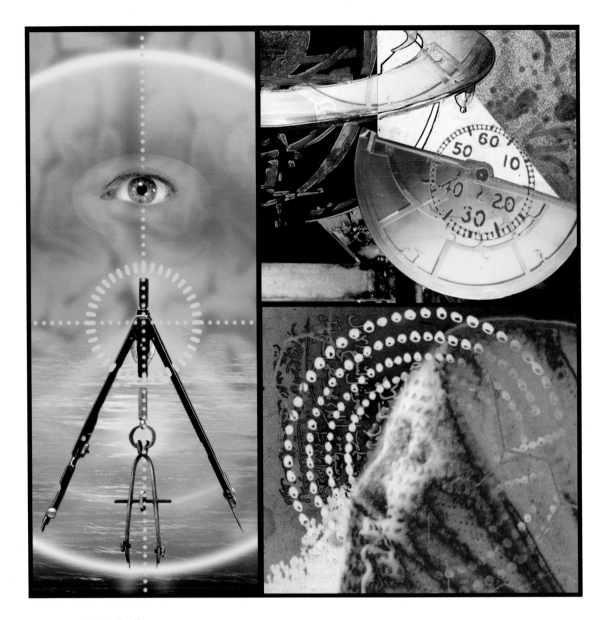

PROJECT: timeXposure
ARTIST: Digital Atelier
PRINTING DEVICE: Roland H-Fi Jet inkjet

Digital Atelier artists Dorothy Simpson Krause, Bonny Lhotka and Karin Schminke used the timeless animated effects of lenticular imaging to present explorations in time, space and light for their work, entitled *timeXposure*.

Multiple interlaced images viewed through a lenticular lens create 3D and multiple images in a single plane. Acting as liaison between the high-tech industry and the fine-art world, the artists strive to explore emerging technologies and provide feedback to developers from the artists' perspective.

From Dorothy Simpson Krause's "Luna" and Bonny Lhotka's "Meridian," Karin Schminke designed "Mindscapes," a lenticular montage of images that reflects transformation through creativity.

The lenticular effect was created using FLIP! Software on an Integraph computer, Roland PetG HighGloss film and Microlens 401pi lenticular lens. Lhotka consulted with Mirage Lenticular Imaging, Montreal, QC, Canada, for proofing. The entire piece entitled *timeXposure* originally appeared with a 60-lpi lens produced by Microlens Technology, Charlotte, NC for the cover of *Signs of the Times* magazine.

Digital Atelier is a registered trademark of Krause, Lhotka, Schminke.

PROJECT: timeXposure "Luna"
ARTIST: Dorothy Simpson Krause
PRINTING DEVICE: Roland H-Fi Jet inkjet

Multiple interlaced images viewed through a lenticular lens create animated, 3D and multiple images in a single plane. This series of work focuses on how we explore the unknown and master our fears. It incorporates symbols, plans for computing devices, molecular drawings, celestial maps, astrological charts and photographs of places of power. Although technology is accused of being "dehumanizing," it is the medium through which the artist attempts to express these most human of needs.

PROJECT: timeXposure "Meridian"
ARTIST: Bonny Lhotka
PRINTING DEVICE: Roland H-Fi Jet inkjet

Multiple interlaced images viewed through a lenticular lens create animated, 3D and multiple images in a single plane. By layering images the artist integrates meanings that invoke a response by the viewer. By looking at the past and responding intuitively, she explores the future by applying knowledge of the present.

PROJECT: (in the name of the) Mother
ARTIST: Dorothy Simpson Krause
PRINTING DEVICE: Encad NovaJet 880 inkjet

Incorporating digital art reproduction techniques into a mix of other components and surface textures can present some striking results. This image was printed in reverse on Rexam Magic white inkjet film, and transferred to a copper surface coated with rabbit-skin glue. Highlights were then scratched and sanded into the copper. The portrait is from a photograph by Emily Taylor.

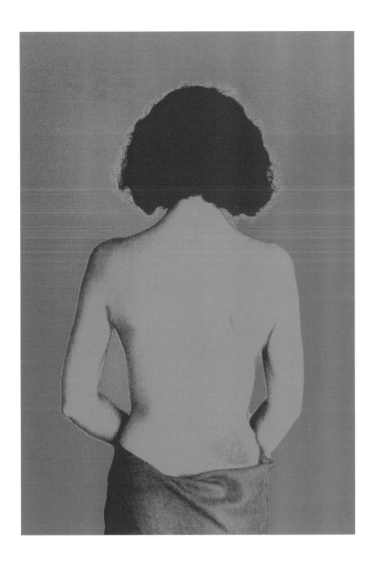

PROJECT: Collection of digital art
ARTIST: Joe Nalven
PRINTING DEVICE: Epson Stylus Pro 1280 and
7500 inkjets

"Digital art" can be either a reproduction of an artist's
original, or a composition comprised of a variety of
elements, brought together and digitally manipulated.
Nalven uses a variety of tools and filters to enhance
scanned photos, and then employs high-resolution
inkjets to print on a mixture of fine-art papers.

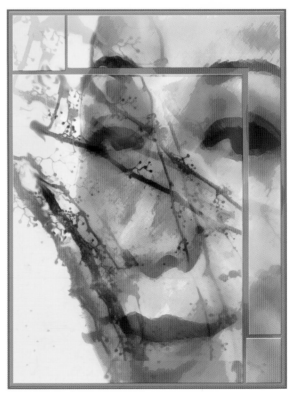

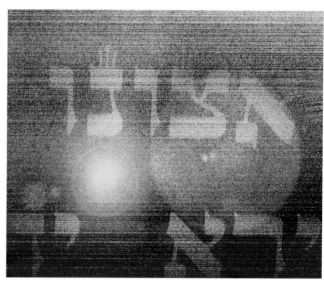

144 The Big Picture

TEXTILE & SPECIALTY APPLICATIONS

Using specialized inks and digital printing and finishing techniques, it's now economically feasible to output a design onto just a few yards of cloth. This makes it possible to create prototypes of new designs as well as customized fashions and home furnishings. It's also possible to create customized carpeting, wallcoverings, ceiling tiles, ceramic tiles, wood and other substrates.

Some companies are using textiles to create graphics for exhibition and retail graphics because the "soft signage" is easy to transport and display. Dye-sublimation techniques are used for more durable soft signage requirements. In inkjet printing, the ink remains on the surface of the fabric or decorated item. In the dye-sublimation process, the specialty inks are converted into gases that permanently fuse into polyester-based or treated fabrics. Textiles created with the dye-sublimation process retain the same feel, drapability, and washability characteristics they had prior to imaging. Inkjet-printed textiles typically must require an extra steaming phase in order to be washable.

PROJECT: DaVinci Exhibit Promotion at Museum of Science, Boston, MA
PRODUCTION: DGI-Invisuals, Burlington, MA
PRINTING DEVICE: Raster Graphics DCS electrostatic system

Boston's Museum of Science commissioned DGI to produce this 9 x 14 ft. lightweight, fabric banner to promote a Leonardo da Vinci exhibit. DGI used the electrostatic dye-sublimation process to create a printed banner that retains the look and feel of the selected fabric.

PROJECT: Fabric Murals at Abbott Laboratories
PRODUCTION: DGI-Invisuals, Burlington, MA
PRINTING DEVICE: Carolina dye-sublimation inkjet

Wall murals created with tensioned, dye-sub-printed fabrics add a warm, gentle touch to the lobby of Abbott Laboratories. DGI used an inkjet dye-sublimation printing process to generate photorealistic images on fire-retardant fabrics. The fabrics were then stretched, mounted, and sewn like pillowcases on custom-manufactured aluminum frames.

PROJECT: "Bean Me Up" Cafe
PRODUCTION: GREGORY, Inc., Buhler, KS
PRINTING DEVICE: Hewlett-Packard 3500 CP wide-format inkjet and MacDermid ColorSpan inkjet

What's unique about this faux-café application is that over 15 different items shown were produced with one type of inkjet media: GREGORY ColorBlast Heat Transfer Media. Inkjet-receptive transfer media can be run through most any inkjet printer, including wide-format machines. Since this product is a "cold peel" after the transfer stage, large items (the wooden table top and the satin wallpaper) are able to receive the image using the heat and pressure of a laminating machine. The next step, after cooling is peeling off the release liner from the inkjet paper to reveal the vivid images. No additional finishing is needed.

Though hard to believe, only a single 36-in. x 60-ft roll of media was used for this entire mock-up. This type of transfer method is popular for one-offs, prototypes and special projects, though it is extremely durable and fade- and water-resistant for long-term applications such as wearables and mousepads.

©2001 Herrmann + Starke

PROJECT: Fisheye Sculpture, Baltimore, MD
PRODUCTION: Hermann + Starke Studios, Insight 180, and Digital Option Center, Baltimore, MD
PRINTING DEVICE: Epson Stylus Pro high-resolution inkjet

A variety of photographs form the colorful, fabric scales on this three-dimensional fish that was part of Baltimore's "Fish Out of Water" community art project. Digital photographer Judy Hermann persuaded 28 fellow members of the local chapter of the American Society of Media Photographers to contribute at least two images. Designers at Insight 180 constructed a layout that incorporated 49 images on one side of the fish, and 60 images on the other. The graphics were output as four 24 x 81-in. panels on Pictorico's inkjet-receptive PolySilk fabric on a wide-format inkjet printer. The image panels were attached to the first structure with a heat-activated adhesive, covered with two coats of a decoupage-process, water-based coating, and then protected with 12 layers of clearcoat.

Photos courtesy of Swirling Silks

PROJECT: Salt Lake City 2002 Olympics & 2002 Paralympics, Salt Lake City, UT
PRODUCTION: Viscotec USA, LLC
PRINTING DEVICE: Direct proprietary inkjet

The Olympic committee assigned a panel of 30 artists and graphic designers to create the images for the many projects needed for the 2002 Olympic and Paralympic events. A total of 417 designs, comprising over 70,000 sq ft of material, were printed. Color consistency, durability, fire-retardance and water resistant finishing all came into play to meet the stringent demands of the Salt Lake City Olympic Committee. Graphic installation included locations such as on the sides of ski slopes, in the speed skating arena, and on the safety pads of the ski jumps.

PROJECT: Thanksgiving Day Parade Floats
PRODUCTION: Northstar Imaging, Troy, MI
PRINTING DEVICE: Vutek UltraVu 5300 superwide inkjet

The Parade Company is an event-services firm that takes pride in being the nation's only
full-service parade company. The company designs, constructs and coordinates all of
the units featured in the annual America's Thanksgiving Parade, in Detroit, MI.
For a recent parade, The Parade Company commissioned Northstar Imaging Solutions
to produce colorful graphics for five floats—some of which were used in Macy's
Thanksgiving Day Parade in New York. The floats promoted the MTV/Nickelodeon TV
series Rugrats; Comcast Cable's Jimmy Neutron character; Marshall Fields department
stores; and the City of Detroit. Because parades provide a fun and effective opportunity
to companies to build public awareness, Northstar Imaging Solutions built a float of its
own for the Detroit parade.

PROJECT: White Light Custom Caskets, Dallas TX
PRINTING DEVICE: Océ Arizona 180 large-format inkjet

An imaginative Dallas radio station manager wanted to add a creative touch to the somberness of funerals by decorating caskets with images that reflect upon the individual's life or interests. Working with a local digital printer, a system was developed and the company 'White Light' was formed. By using a custom Photoshop template, designers can prepare the theme or collection of images to fit exactly as needed.
The file is printed on adhesive-backed vinyl, cut to shape, and then applied to the 12-gauge aluminum casket.

Designs from custom to ready-made, range from religious icons to NASCAR to Native American images. Shown here are the popular "Fairway to Heaven" model, and a custom order done for an Elvis fan emblazoned "Return to Sender."

PROJECT: ThunderCoat Jacket
PRODUCTION: Bonny Lhotka, Lhotka Studio/silkRiversilk, Boulder, CO
PRINTING DEVICE: Mutoh Falcon inkjet

The ThunderCoat design originated from one of Bonny Lhotka's acrylic paint-ings. The 48 x 48-in. painting was scanned on an Eclipse flatbed scanner and designed by Doug Komhyr of Boulder, CO. A local blueprint shop scanned a garment pattern. The images were created in Adobe Photoshop to fit the pattern design.

Next, Lhotka printed the designs onto 5 yds of paper-backed Jacquard 23mm (0.9-in.) Silk Charmeuse inkjet fabric on the Mutoh Falcon RJ- 8000 inkjet printer at 720 x 720 dpi using the Wasatch SoftRip. After the paper back-ing was removed, the silk was rolled in tissue paper and steamed to heat-set the dye. After an hour of steaming per yard, the fabric was unrolled and the material washed to remove excess dye. Then Lhotka squeezed the water out in a towel and ironed the fabric until dry. Seamstress Laura Simmons of Extraordinaire Fine Clothing, Boulder, CO, cut and sewed the pieces from the fabric. Lhotka used Lyson Reactive Digital Textile Ink for this series.

This coat reflects the designer's desire to express the individuality of each garment in the silkRiversilk Collection. As an innovator and recipient of the Computer World Smithsonian Technology Award and Kodak's Innovator Award 2001, Lhotka has created the silkRiversilk Collection as a state of the art entry into the accessory market as a collectable customizable item.

PROJECT: Dye-Sublimation Gallery
PRODUCTION: Dream Interiors, division of Specialty Toner Corporation (STC)
PRINTING DEVICE: Raster Graphics 5442 electrostatic printer with STC's kV Color dye-sublimation inks

As a forerunner and key developer of the electrostatic dye-sublimation market, Specialty Toner Corporation (STC) developed a 5-color set of toners to expand the color gamut of dye-sublimation printing to rival that of 6-color inkjets. The Dream Interiors division of STC has created a gallery of items like some seen here to show the interior design market what can be done with digital textile printing. In addition to this, electrostatic dye-sub printing can be, and is used, for producing outdoor-durable graphics.

PROJECT: Corona Light Sculpture Unit
PRODUCTION: Forest Corporation, Twinsburg, OH
PRINTING DEVICE: Océ Arizona 180 inkjet

This light sculpture unit is a prototype that was used to promote larger production runs to Corona's marketing group. Digital printing is an ideal technology for prototyping graphics and applications to show clients what a new promotional piece can offer to a market-place, while giving them a genuine sample of what the final product will look like.

PROJECT: Vamp Shoes
PRODUCTION: Herrmann + Starke Digital Photography
PRINTING DEVICE: Epson 1280 desktop inkjet

Using Pictorico PolySilk inkjet-printable fabric, the "face" pattern
was printed and then cut to fit the three-dimensional shape of the
shoe and heel. Fabric adhesive was used to adhere the material.
Originally created for an exhibition of digital photography featuring
works by members of Olympus' Camedia Masters Program, these
shoes were subsequently featured in *American Photo* magazine
and exhibited at various venues throughout the year.

PROJECT: Product Launch Banners at FAO Schwarz, New York, NY
PRODUCTION: Color Envision, Inc., New York, NY
PRINTING DEVICE: High-resolution large-format inkjet

These banners, spotlighting Asia's answer to Mattel's Barbie doll, decorated the aisles of the FAO Schwarz toy store when China's Yue-Sai company launched its Yue-Sai Wa Wa dolls in the US. In keeping with the stylish look of an international fashion doll, the banners were produced at the Color Envision digital art studio on an inkjet-printable poly-taffeta fabric from Jacquard Ink Jet Fabric Systems.

PROJECT: Event Signage for DIFFA Fundraiser, New York, NY
PRODUCTION: Color Envision, Inc., New York, NY
PRINTING DEVICE: High-resolution large-format inkjet

This striking, free-standing display greeted guests at the Viva Glam Casino fundraiser held at Cipriani on 42nd St. for the Design Industries Foundation Fighting AIDS (DIFFA). For an elegant touch, the graphic was output on an inkjet-receptive crepe-de-chine from Jacquard Ink Jet Fabric Systems.

After the paper-backed fabric was fed through the wide-format inkjet printer, the paper backing was removed and panels were sewn together, with hemmed pockets at the edges for the display-stand poles.

PROJECT: Grimoldi Watch Banners in Torneau Time Machine Store, New York, NY
PRODUCTION: Color Envision, Inc.; Quinto + Co., New York, NY
PRINTING DEVICE: High-resolution inkjet

These elegant, crepe-de-chine and silk-satin banners were created to herald the availability of prestigious, Italian-made Grimoldi watches in the four-story Torneau Time Machine watch superstore. The banners were designed by Quinto + Co. and output at Color Envision on inkjet-receptive, paper-backed fabrics supplied by Jacquard Fabric Ink Jet Systems. After the banners were printed, the paper backing was removed. For quick removal after the promotion was over, the banners were hung with wires, rope and Velcro®.

DIRECTORY OF CONTRIBUTORS

AAA FLAG & BANNER
Los Angeles, CA
www.aaaflag.com

ABI AIRBRUSH IMAGES
Conroe, TX
www.airbrushimages.com

ADERA CORPORATION
Las Vegas, NV
www.aderacorp.com

ADLER DISPLAY
Baltimore, MD
www.adlerdisplay.com

ADMART INTERNATIONAL
Danville, KY
www.admart.com

AGREDA COMMUNICATIONS
Cutten, CA
www.agreda.com

AK FLAG & BANNER
Little Rock, AR
www.flagandbanner.com

ALKIT DIGITAL IMAGING
New York, NY
www.alkit.com/adi

AMERICA'S CUP MEDIA
Sausalito, CA
www.americascupmedia.com

ANDRÉS IMAGING & GRAPHICS
Chicago, IL
www.andresimaging.com

ARKANSAS FLAG AND BANNER
Little Rock, AR
503-375-7633

BIG APPLE VISUAL GROUP
New York, NY
www.bigapplesign.com

BURTON IMAGING GROUP
Philadelphia, PA
www.burtonimaging.com

CHRISTOPHER CHADBOURNE AND ASSOCIATES
Cambridge MA
617-547-5330

THE COLLEGE KIT
Lebanon, NH
www.collegekit.com

COLOR BY PERGAMENT
New York, NY
www.color-by-pergament.com

COLOR ENVISION INC.
New York, NY
www.colorenvision.com

COLOR X
New York, NY
www.color-x.com

COMMUNICATION ARTS
Boulder, CO
www.commarts-boulder.com

THE CREATIS GROUP
San Francisco, CA
www.creatisgroup.com

DGI-INVISUALS
Burlington, MA
www.dgiusa.com

DLM STUDIO
Cleveland, OH
www.dlmstudio.com

DEEP DESIGN
Atlanta, GA
www.deepdesign.com

DIGITAL ATELIER
www.digitalatelier.com

DIGITAL OPTION CENTER
Baltimore, MD
410-467-9159

THE DIGITAL PRINTING CENTER
Chicago, IL
www.dp-center.com

DISPLAY PRESENTATIONS LTD
Hauppage, NY.
www.displaypresentations.com

DREAM INTERIORS
See Specialty Toner Corporation

E.B. LUCE CORPORATION
Worcester, MA
www.ebluce.com

ESTRIA
See TRANSISTOR 6

EXTRALARGE GRAPHICS ITALIA
See VERTICAL VISION INTERNATIONAL

EXTREME ADVERTISING & PROMOTION
New York, NY
Ericfextreme@aol.com

FASTSIGNS
Cleveland, OH
www.fastsigns.com

FERRARI COLOR INC.
Sacramento, CA
www.ferraricolor.com

FLEMING & ROSKELLY INC.
Newport, RI
www.comresults.com

FOREST CORPORATION
Twinsburg, OH
www.forestcorporation.com

FREECAR MEDIA
Los Angeles, CA
www.FreeCarMedia.com

FREELANCE LETTERING INC.
Indianapolis, IN 46222
www.freelancelettering.com

GES EXPOSITION SERVICES
San Francisco, CA
www.gesexpo.com

GERON ASSOCIATES
Markham, ON Canada
www.geron.ca

GIANT IMPRESSIONS
Santa Clara, CA
www.giantimpressions.com

GILBERT, INA
Toronto, ON Canada
416-297-8002
http://home.istar.ca/~cintar/inaspage/ina.html

GORDON SIGN
Denver, CO
www.gordonsign.com

GRAPHIC INNOVATIONS
Providence, RI
www.graphinn.com

GRAPHIC SYSTEMS INSTALLERS INC.
Lakeland, FL
www.graphicinstallers.com

GREGORY INC.
Buhler, KS
www.gregory1.com

HERMANN & STARKE DIGITAL PHOTOGRAPHY
Elliott City, MD
www.HSStudio.com

HUNT DESIGN ASSOCIATES
Pasadena, CA
www.huntdesign.com

ICON DIGITAL PRODUCTIONS
Richmond Hill, ON, Canada
www.iconprint.com

IG3 INTEGRATED GRAPHICS
Vaughan, ON, Canada
www.ig3.com

IMAGIC
Hollywood, CA
www.imagicla.com

INOVA EXHIBIT PROJECTS
Mount Laurel, NJ
www.inovaexhibits.com

INSIGHT 180
Ellicott City, MD
www.insight180.com

KIKU OBATA & COMPANY
St. Louis, MO
www.kikuobata.com

KRAUSE, DOROTHY SIMPSON
Marshfield Hills, MA
www.DotKrause.com

LHOTKA STUDIO
Boulder, CO
www.lhotka.com

LOGICA DESIGN INC.
Providence, RI
www.logicadesign.com

MAKOM/M.NUR MARKETING & KOMMUNIKATION GMBH
Kassel, Germany
www.makom.de

MANDEL, MYRA
Moshov, Homed, Israel
www.artfromthewell.com

MCCANN ERICKSON-SEATTLE
Seattle, WA
www.me-seattle.com

MEGA MEDIA CONCEPTS LTD.
Springfield, VA
631-325-5929

METROMEDIA TECHNOLOGIES (MMT)
New York, NY
www.mmtglobal.com

MICROLENS TECHNOLOGY
Matthews, NC
www.microlens.com

MURPHY AND COMPANY
Los Angeles, CA
www.murphyand.com

NALVEN, JOE
Poway, CA
www.digitalartist1.com

NEW IMAGE TECHNOLOGIES
South Elgin, IL
nuimagetek@aol.com

NITE-BRIGHT SIGNS
Ft. Myers, FL
www.nitebright.com

NORTHSTAR IMAGING SOLUTIONS
Troy, MI
248-588-4400

NOTRE MONDE
Columbus, OH
614-263-7708

OMNIGRAPHICS
Sandton, South Africa
www.omnigraphics.co.za

ONPOINT VISUALS
Boston, MA
www.onpointvisuals.com

OPTIMA GRAPHICS
Fenton, MO
www.optimagfx.com

PCL GRAPHICS
Toronto, ON, Canada
www.pclgraphics.com

PASQUARELLI, RICHARD
New York, NY
212-2267221
pasquarelli@rcn.com

PICTOGRAPHICS
Las Vegas, NV
www.pictographics.net

POWER GRAPHICS
Salt Lake City, UT
www.power-graphics.com

PRATT SCREEN AND DIGITAL PRODUCTION
Indianapolis, IN
www.prattcorp.com

QUINTO + COMPANY
New York, NY
www.quinto.com

THE RDW GROUP
Providence, RI
www.rdwgroup.com

RETAIL PLANNING ASSOCIATES
Columbus, OH
www.rpaworldwide.com

ROBERTS, CHARLIE
Lawrence, KS
620-960-0665

SCHMINKE, KARIN
Kenmore, WA
425-402-8606
www.schminke.com

SCIENCE MUSEUM OF MINNESOTA
Saint Paul, MN
www.smm.org

SHEA ARCHITECTS INC.
Minneapolis, MN
612-339-2257

SIGN ART INC.
Charlotte, NC
704-597-9801

SKYTAG
Beverly Hills, CA
www.skytag.net

SPARKS EXHIBITS & ENVIRONMENTS
Philadelphia, PA
www.sparksonline.com

SPECIALTY TONER CORPORATION (STC),
DREAM INTERIORS
www.specialtytoner.com

STEIN, BARRY
Cookeville, TN
www.BsteinArt.com

SUNGRAF
Hallandale, FL
www.sungraf.com

SUPERGRAPHICS
Seattle, WA and San Jose, CA
www.supergraphics.com

TELLURIDE FILM FESTIVAL PRODUCTION CREW
Transue, Garry, Art Director, Blammo Lab
Sonoma, CA
707-996-6386

TOTALLY CUSTOM WALLPAPER
Atlanta, GA
888-458-9255
www.totallycustomwallpaper.com

TRANSITOR 6, ESTRA (artist)
Oakland, CA
www.transistor6.com

TDI (TRANSPORATION DISPLAYS INC.)
San Francisco, CA
www.tdiworldwide.com

TYPICO MEGAPRINTS GMBH
Lochal, Austria
www.typico.com

VERTICAL VISION INTERNATIONAL/
EXTRALARGE GRAPHICS ITALIA
www.verticalvision.info

VISCOTEC, USA
New York, NY
212-216-9523

VISUAL IMPRESSIONS
Charlotte, NC
www.visualimpressionsonline.com

VOMELA SPECIALTIES COMPANY
St Paul, MN 55107
www.vomela.com

WEST OFFICE EXHIBITION DESIGN
Oakland, CA
www.woed.com

WHITE LIGHT
Dallas, TX
www.artcaskets.com

WILLIAMS GRAPHIC
Sylmar, CA
818-365-9899

WYATT DESIGN GROUP INC.
Pasadena, CA
www.wyattdesigngroup.com

YABU PUSHELBERG
Toronto, ON, Canada
www.yabupushelberg.com

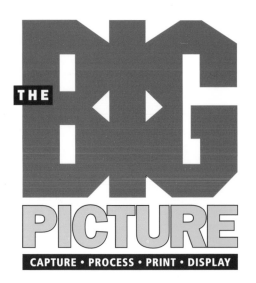

Intelligence in Visual Communications

The Big Picture is about so much more than large-format digital printing. Appealing to content creators as well as output suppliers, we cover all phases of visual communications.

capture   process   print   display

www.bigpicture.net

ST Media Group International Inc.
407 Gilbert Avenue
Cincinnati, Ohio 45202
USA
www.stmediagroup.com

In Every Issue

Updates on Equipment, Systems, Supplies and Trends: Our product update section highlights inkjet printers, photo imagers, inks, media, laminating films, mounting supplies, digital cameras, scanners, software, color management tools, workstations, storage, file-transfer options, applications, finishing equipment and supplies, and display systems. We also spotlight and explain emerging trends in application and technology.

Digital Portfolio is a showcase section that introduces designers and graphics buyers to creative suppliers and out-of-home advertising, P-O-P displays, vehicle graphics, photography, and fine-art reproduction. Case studies highlight how specific systems and supplies are being used in real-world applications.

Resources presents news about specialized services, reports, websites, training programs, product catalogs, technical support, and publications.